SPIRIT OF THE SEA

SPIRIT OF THE SEA

MARIE-FRANCE BOYER

WITH 147 ILLUSTRATIONS, 131 IN COLOR

Thames & Hudson

I DEDICATE THIS BOOK TO ALL THOSE WHO LOVE WANDERING AROUND HARBOURS AND ALONG THE SHORE.

TO THOSE WHO KNOW HOW TO CLEAN FISH AND PICK WHELKS FROM THEIR SHELLS.

TO THOSE WHO LOVE THE SMELL OF SILT AND SEAWEED AND UNDERSTAND THE POETRY OF NETS AND LOBSTER POTS.

TO ALL THOSE, FINALLY, WHOSE BAGGAGE IS ALWAYS WEIGHED DOWN WITH STONES FROM THE BEACH,

AND WHO DON'T WAIT FOR FINE WEATHER BEFORE THEY VENTURE OUT.

DESIGNED BY MICHAEL TIGHE

Translated from the French by Barbara Mellor

First published in hardcover in the United States of America in 2003 by Thames & Hudson Inc., 500 Fifth Avenue, New York, New York 10110

thamesandhudsonusa.com

Library of Congress Catalog Card Number 2002107854
ISBN 0-500-51103-9

Printed and bound in Singapore by Tien Wah Press

Half title: painted tin lobster, United States.
Page 2: fisherman's cottage, Brittany.
Title page: swordfish.
Pages 4–5: abandoned net with dandelions.
This page, background: English fisherman, 1905.
Pages 8–9: huts on the Blyth estuary, near Southwold in Suffolk.
Pages 10–11: Ile Molène, Brittany.

CONTENTS

HERRING
NETS
£25
Manila Rope
SORCERESS

LT 10
FRESH
FISH
OPEN
1030

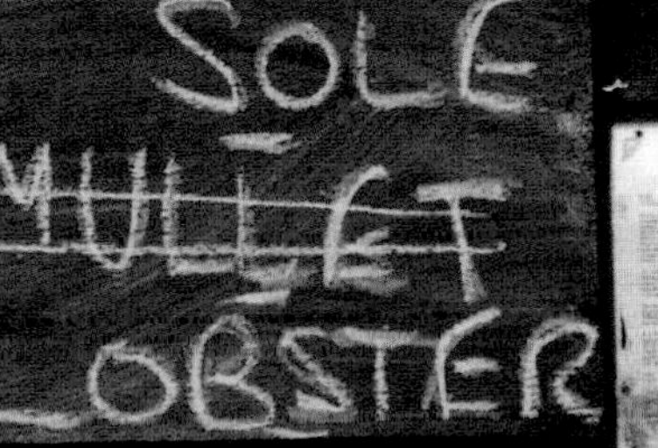
CAUGHT TODAY
SEA BASS
SEA TROUT
DOVER
SOLE
MULLET
LOBSTER

TRADITIONAL SAILING CHARTER
'GIRL SYBIL'
SAIL SOUTHWOLD
& THE HERITAGE COAST

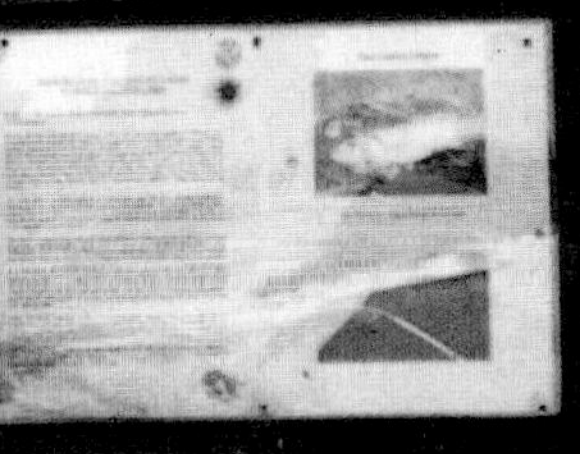

PROPERTY P.A.S.
LOWESTOFT

One day, in a school in the outskirts of Paris, a teacher asked her pupils to draw a fish. One child, clearly baffled by the request, eventually drew an oblong – the shape of the slabs of frozen cod that his mother bought at the supermarket. We are in danger of forgetting that fish come from the sea, and that to fish for them you need a boat.

Day after day, aboard trawlers in bright paintbox blues, greens or reds, their decks piled with oddly shaped objects made of wood, plastic, chain and rope, fishermen haul in their catch of sea creatures – slimy or covered in spines, torpedo-shaped or flat, slippery or scaly, magnificent or monstrous. These creatures have formed part of the human diet since the beginning of time. Nevertheless, living unseen by us under the sea in hidden deeps, fish and crustaceans are less familiar to most of us than the cows, chicken and sheep that also end their days as food on our dinner plates.

PREFACE

Fish, fishing boats and fishermen all constitute a world apart. Those who like to wander around harbours and along the shore will recognize its traces, and will appreciate the colourful objects that punctuate its landscape, so familiar and yet so full of poetry – lifebuoys, oilskins and piles of nets and lobster pots, which to contemporary eyes look like so many artistic installations of the *arte povera* movement. They will also be acquainted with the improbably picturesque institutions that small-scale coastal fishing brings to the shore in its wake: not only the cafés, fish auctions and fishmongers, but also the seamen's chapels and Lilliputian museums.

These days, deep-sea fishing is an increasingly rare activity, the preserve of factory-ships equipped with everything necessary to slice, chop, freeze and process the catch. These ships stay at sea for months, leaving the harbours empty and abandoned.

At the same time, marine life is being fished to exhaustion – stocks of halibut, tuna and cod have halved in the last fifty years – and to find fish the boats must go out further and further, fishing ever deeper waters. Every country is now required to respect the quotas that have been laid down, as well as specific fishing zones. Necessary as they are, these measures are disastrous for fishing communities. Yet scattered along the coasts of the Atlantic Ocean, the English Channel and the North Sea, from Stonington in the state of Maine, USA, to Lowestoft in Suffolk, from Biarritz in south-west France to Le Conquet in Brittany, there is still a repertoire of images, handed down from past generations of fishermen, that are as pleasing to the eye as to the imagination. This harsh and distinctive world is made up of a thousand details – the lament of the Portuguese *fado* and the cry of seagulls, the boom of a foghorn and the splash made by dropping anchor, the name a fisherman gives his boat and the décor of old fishmongers' shops, the brilliant silky colours of nets and odd-looking fish. This is a perilous place, where fishermen entrust their safety to their instincts and their knowledge of the sea, always at risk from the elements and their potentially murderous violence. This is a theatre in which all is on a vast scale, all is shot through with griefs and passions. And, of course, we are not concerned here with the Mediterranean, the Pacific or the Caribbean, but rather with cold seas – more often grey than turquoise, more often pulsing with a heavy swell than calm as glass, and bordered by coastlines of granite and schist that stretch beside the shores of the Atlantic, the Channel and all along the North Sea. This world of shifting half-tones does not readily reveal itself, and yet it imprints its spirit on every coast: every port and harbour has it heroes, its ordinary people and its stars, and it is through them that the old legends and superstitions, myths and rituals live on.

Page 13: on 21 June, the summer solstice and the feast of St John, the fishermen of Biarritz in south-west France put up new cross-shaped bouquets of *Cineraria maritima* to protect their *crampottes*, or huts, against bad luck.

Opposite: a trawler off the Shetlands in Scotland . 'If people realized what we are doing to the sea they would be scandalized,' remarks one of the fishermen. 'It's as if farmers were bulldozing the whole of the countryside. But it's happening under the water, so nobody cares.'

Practically all the old rigged boats, those magnificent vessels with their great sails of faded cotton that so inspired painters, have now disappeared. In France, however, there are still some ten thousand fishermen, in the UK around fifteen thousand, who own their own boats and work in the old way, leaving harbour at dawn, fishing close to the coast, and returning at the end of the day. There are still modest-sized boats, small clinker-built vessels that are winched ashore or dragged up by tractors or even by muscle power, such as the *flobards* of the Boulogne coastline, the *caïques* of Yport in Normandy and the traditional fishing boats of Hastings in Sussex. But the most common nowadays are drifters and trawlers, their decks cleared for stacks of lobster pots. They are an unforgettable sight leaving harbour at dawn, engines chugging, looking festive with multicoloured pennants and pink plastic floats – the modern

THE BOATS

version of cork floats, old tyres and glass balls in nets. The boats are the fishermen's cherished possessions and their names are always chosen with care. English names for boats range from *Rosie Haze* to *Our Lady.* In France, there are fewer and fewer named *Pieuse paysanne* (Pious Countrywoman), *Confiance en Dieu* (Trust in God), *Enfant des houles* (Child of the Swell) and *Angélus de la mer* (Angelus of the Sea). On the other hand, on the Breton coast between the Côtes d'Armor and the Morbihan, Breton names such as *Gwen en Mar* (Sea Spray) and *Men Du* (Black Stone) are becoming popular. Such classics as *Gildas-Loïc* and *Marie-Georges* are still to be seen, and *Korrigan* (Goblin), *Espadon* (Swordfish), and especially *Loup de mer* (Old Salt) and *Etoile des Flots* (Star of the Waves), have withstood the ebb and flow of passing fashions, as if to remind us that some dreams go on for ever.

PÉPÉ LOUIS

ST BENOIT
BOULOGNE

OUR PAM AND PETER
HASTINGS PORT OF RYE

MARIE ANDR
BOU

VERONIQU
GNE

ROSIE
HAZE

COTE
D'OPALE

Etoile de mer
DK
Sandra 
Our Lady 
72 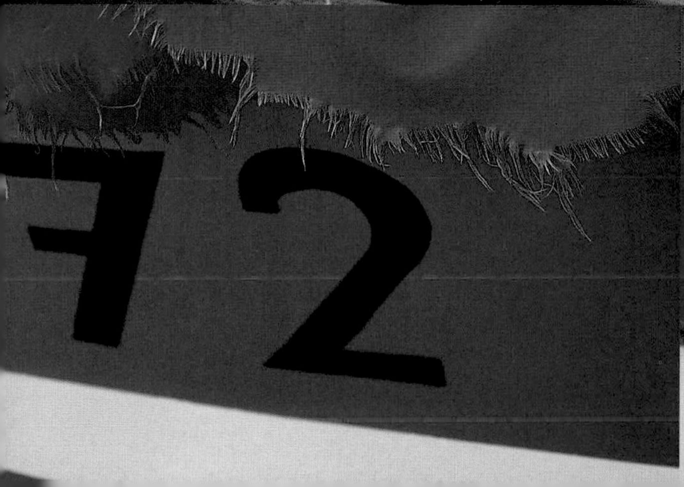
L'★ du Nord

Page 17: the *Pépé Louis* (Grandpa Louis). *Preceding pages*: the graphic layers of names painted and repainted countless times. *These pages*: a stern trawler *(opposite)* and a crabber.

Among the world's workers, fishermen are a breed apart. Like those who work the soil, they have a close and now rare understanding of nature. Fishing is as subject to the capriciousness of the weather as are the harvests on land, but fishermen are more exposed because their lives and the tools of their trade are also directly threatened by the elements. Storms blow up without warning, and sometimes they are killers. 'We fear the sea because we know what it can do,' declares a fisherman from L'Aber-Wrach in Finistère, Brittany. 'No one hides the fact that they're afraid.' In order to deal with this constant danger and lurking fear, fishermen support themselves with superstitions and extraordinary tales of the exploits of seafaring heroes whose courage and gallantry are the pride and honour of the fishing community.

Fame and reputation begin with a nickname. At Cromer in Norfolk, fishermen are

THE FISHERMEN

known as 'Crabs', while their 'rivals' a few miles along the coast at Sheringham are 'Shannocks'. Their colleagues in Hastings, meanwhile, are called 'Tan Frocks'. In the port there is always someone like a Quiddy Mitchell, a Woody Woodgale or a Pierre le Rouge (Red Peter). 'Anchor Willie had a close shave,' recounts a sailor. 'As he was dropping anchor he fell overboard, and next thing he knew he was a hundred feet down with the chain wrapped round his ankle. Fortunately the captain raised it up again quick as he could. Willie was bleeding from the ears when they brought him up, but he lived for another fifty years at least . . . .' And so a hero was born. 'Sardine John', on the other hand, 'stayed down for good when the buttons of the old coat he had flung on got tangled in the mesh of a lobster pot.' Everyone who lives in a fishing port can recount dozens of stories like this.

Page 23: a 1901 portrait of Onésime Frébourg, who in the early years of the last century saved the lives of some fifty seafarers. His chestful of medals testifies to his status as hero. *Opposite and left*: designed to offer protection against wind, rain, sea-spray and sun, fishermen's working clothes – jerseys, oilskins, dungarees, cloth jackets and caps – also confer a certain stylishness on their wearers. Oilskins are traditionally bright yellow, so that any man accidentally falling overboard can be spotted more easily in the water.

Fishermen in the early 20th century wore 'overalls' of oiled or tarred cotton which they tied around their waists *(right)*. Buttons could get entangled in ropes, and so were forbidden at sea. Heavy and stiff, these garments restricted movement and were cumbersome to wear.

In the 1960s, a new and much lighter type of oilskin made of coated synthetic fabric was produced, with welded seams and zip or Velcro fastenings. Rubber boots had already replaced the traditional heavy wooden clogs and leather gaiters *(above)*.

In a different genre of fishing, the angler who struggles to reel in a sea bass is another type of 'superman', capable of going out to sea in conditions when everyone else would judge it more prudent to stay ashore. Sea bass favour rocky reefs, dangerous eddies and the most treacherous of currents. Whenever they come across a shoal of small fish, their carnivorous nature betrays them. Like the wolf, *le loup* (one of the French names of the sea bass), they hurl themselves on their prey, alerting sea birds who dive into the water, in turn attracting the attention of any sea anglers in the vicinity. Standing legs braced with one hand on the throttle and the other gripping his fishing rod, the angler is aware that the slightest error could smash his boat and lose him everything – yet, on a good day, he could reel in 160 kilos (350 lb) of fish in three hours. 'For me the sea is everything, it's my revenge on life,' admits one.

Opposite: in Suffolk, the Maritime Museum in Lowestoft – the most easterly port in Britain, home to a fishing fleet of a thousand boats in 1920 – is housed in a flint cottage overlooking the sea. Its displays include models of fishing boats, demonstrations of different fishing techniques, and even a life-size replica of the aft cabin of a steam drifter showing the crew's quarters.

The most celebrated heroes of all are the lifeboat men, often fishermen or retired sailors themselves. Unpaid volunteers, they are constantly on standby. They are ready to confront the elements and push beyond the limits of the possible. 'We are one hundred per cent motivated. You wouldn't hesitate to rescue even your worst enemy from the sea.' H. F. Bailey of Cromer saved 818 lives, and as great a number of seamen owed their survival to Onésime Frébourg of Fécamp. Some of these heroes had whole chestfuls of medals. Yet sometimes the sea is the final victor. François Morin of Finistère drowned while fishing, great lifesaver though he was. His name is now legendary, and his daughter Violette never tires of describing how her 'great man' of a father had earned so many medals that on official occasions the weight would drag his jersey down around his knees. There are portraits of some of these heroes in such museums as the Musée des Terre-Neuvas in Fécamp or the Maritime Museum in Lowestoft which give a wonderfully evocative picture of the lives of these 'hardy old salts'.

FISHERMANS SEA BISCUIT
MADE BY W.B. COOPER 1934
PRESENTED BY SKIPPER WALTER
SPORE

SARAH & ANN
MARITIME MUSEUM

Since (in the words of a Norfolk seaman) the wind doesn't 'blow round them but through them', fishermen have for many years worn the traditional seaman's jersey in oiled wool. In France, the Breton fisherman's jersey, navy blue, buttoned on the left shoulder and originally part of the uniform of the French Navy, is close-fitting so as not to impede movement. Ireland is famous for its Aran sweaters with their tremendous range of stitches. Norfolk 'Gansey' sweaters *(left and opposite)*, inspired by their Guernsey equivalents, have been worn since the 17th century, and are recognizable by their 'chimney' neck and the fact that they were made in a single piece. Traditionally knitted by fishermen's wives, they feature a variety of motifs, including the Tree of Life, bees, diamonds, anchors and symbolic rope designs. Every fishing family once had its own combination of stitches and patterns, which in the saddest circumstances could serve to identify the bodies of drowned men.

Fish are enigmatic creatures. Whenever a fisherman lands an exceptional catch – and occasionally there is a veritable monster or a 'freak' – it is immediately seen as an embodiment of the immensity of the ocean, its unplumbed depths, and the obscure dread – as well as the delight – that it stirs in us all. Fish represent the unfathomable mystery of the sea, and the sea itself thrives on such prodigies. People believed in mermaids for centuries, after all. In Norway, it used to be thought that the aurora borealis, or northern lights, were the reflection of a shoal of herring, affectionately known in the north of England as King Herring or silver darlin' because of the wealth that came in their wake. There are some events that remain inexplicable, moreover, such as the tragic disappearance on two occasions of the shoals of sardines that were the staple industry around the Bay of Concarneau, north-west of Lorient in Finistère.

THE CATCH

Between 1880 and 1887 and again between 1902 and 1907, the capricious habits of this tiny blue fish plunged the region into poverty, forced thousands of seamen down the mines, and shut down canning factories, boatyards and rope factories. Even though we now know that fish migrations are partly a result of reproduction and feeding habits, such phenomena still take us by surprise. If a certain species is no longer visible near the surface, it could simply have taken refuge in deeper waters.

Each species requires different conditions for spawning, including a specific water temperature and degree of salinity. Herring, sardines and cod all lay eggs that are fertilized externally, and swim in shoals, belly to belly, to their favoured spawning grounds. The tuna – the largest fish in the Atlantic after the swordfish – is so exhausted and emaciated after spawning, that it can devour up to a hundred

Preceding pages: sardines in a canning factory. *Right and below*: workers in the early 20th-century fishing industry. Little can match a fisherman's pride when he lands an exceptional catch. A lobster may be 'as big as a

four-year-old child'; a tuna may weigh 800 kilos (1,750 lbs) – this one caught from a boat out of Folkestone was 347 kilos (694 lbs). Occasionally, a whale expires on a Breton beach: a momentous event.

Thon géant capturé
le 22 Septembre 1910 par le
Dundee Sainte-Marie, du Port de
Folkestone. Pois total : 694 livres.
Acheté par M. Bourbiel, concessionnaire d
Julien Damoy à Champagne-sur-Seine, et d
l'Hôtel du Cheval Noir (J. Marcère, propriét

347 KILOGS
issements
Moret à

mackerel an hour. A great predator, it roams the seas in search of its fishy prey: anchovies, herrings and sardines. In June, it leaves the Atlantic and makes for the Mediterranean to spawn – even if, as is the case with those that set out from Scotland or Senegal, this means a journey of hundreds of miles. The tuna is an athletic swimmer, capable of covering distances of over thirty kilometres (twenty miles) a day. In contrast, the ray, a strange lozenge-shaped fish with its mouth on its abdomen, does not migrate. The male has an external organ at the point where his tail joins his body, which he uses to fertilize the female, pinning her against the sand of the ocean floor with his fins, the powerful, undulating 'wings' that he also uses to suffocate his prey. Sea bass prefer sparkling water, full of oxygen, and they gravitate to areas of turbulence, while gilt-head bream prefer still water.

The angler-fish or monkfish, which the French call *crapaud* (toad) or *diable des mers* (sea devil), is not, alas, blessed with good looks. At the fishmongers' it is displayed like a joint of meat, minus both skin and head, so that its sliminess and its huge voracious mouth, garnished with teeth and bristling with spikes, doesn't put off customers. The grenadier fish and swordfish, deep-sea species that have only recently appeared on our plates, look equally daunting to shoppers, who in this age of convenience foods know little about fish. In the bar of the TGV, the high-speed train, from Brest to Paris, a young man was heard talking to a traveller some years his senior. Explaining that he was in sales for a Vietnamese company based on the Mekong river, he boasted that his wares were 'the fish of the future: no bones, no tail, no head, no fat, no smell, no skin and no taste! It's what everyone wants nowadays.' 'My father had a restaurant with a Michelin star,' was the riposte. 'Nowadays people have forgotten how to eat. Give me a sea bass, a bunch of shallots and some good demi-sel butter, and then you'll have something to write home about!'

Preceding pages: salt cod drying on the Norwegian Lofoten Islands. The cod is salted then wind-dried on tall hurdles which look like fragile and spectacular wooden cathedrals.
Right: in Normandy and Brittany and on British coasts, there are fishermen who sell their catch fresh from the sea, either on the quay beside their boats or on rickety roadside stalls.

Left: stocks of salt cod in Norway. The plump, tapering fish are cut in two before being salted and dried. Piled on wooden palettes, the fish resemble tottering piles of parchment. *Below*: until the 1960s, the fishermen of Fécamp went on an annual migration every February to Iceland or Newfoundland, where they spent long months fishing for cod in inhuman conditions. At that time, the economy of the entire coastline depended on these expeditions.

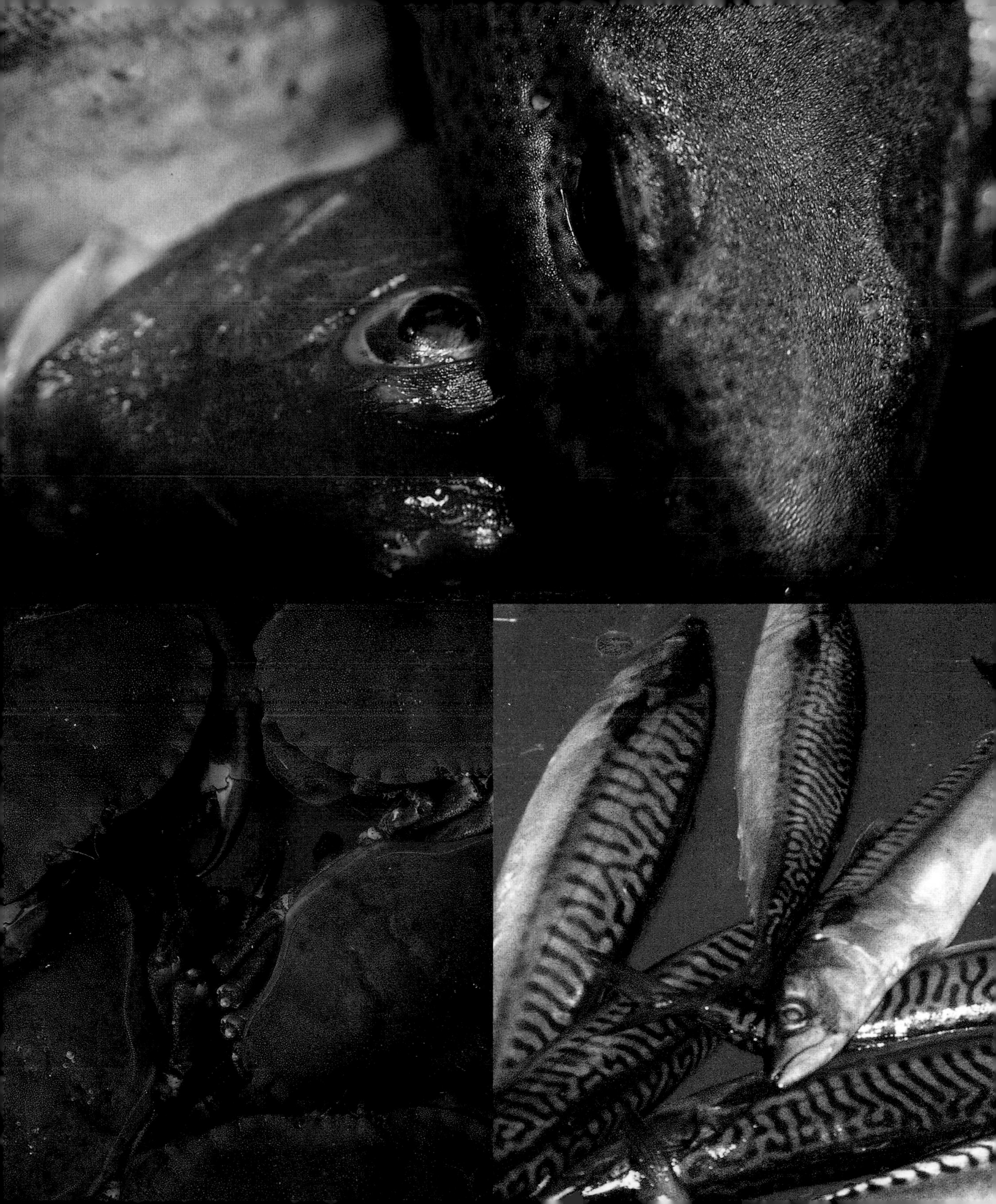

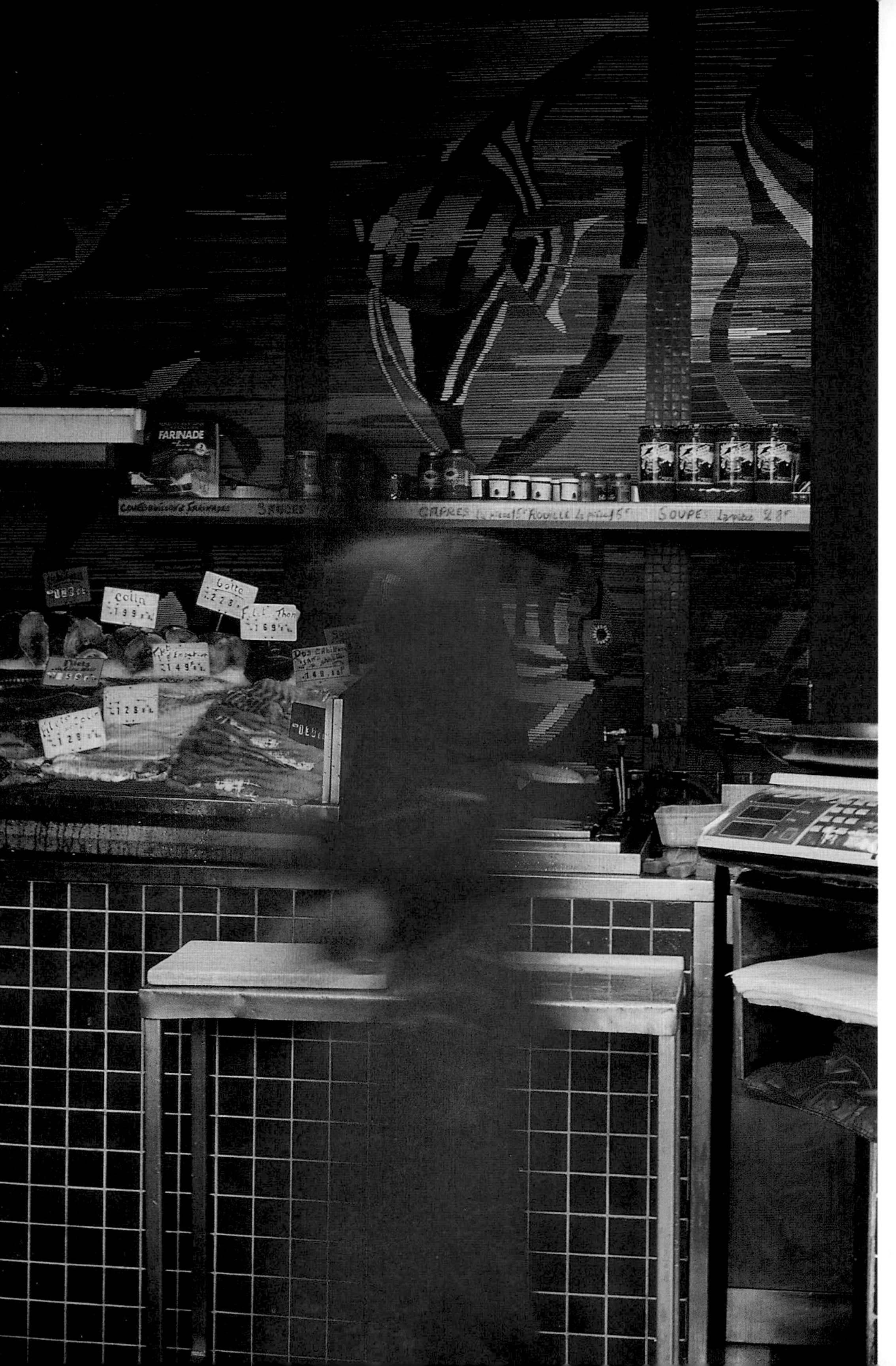

Preceding pages, clockwise from top left: scallops, herring fillets, gurnard and dogfish (huss), mackerel, edible crabs and gilt-head bream.
These pages: the fish shop *La Marée à Paris* (The Paris Catch), formerly known as *A la carpe frétillante* (The Frisky Carp). Today's fishmongers tend to favour rather bland, antiseptic décor. In the past, walls would be covered with colourful mosaics, while the fish and shellfish were arranged in imaginative displays against a background of fishing nets, floats, plastic flowers and decoratively cut lemons. The fabulous displays still to be seen in the Food Hall of Harrods in London, reminiscent of the 16th-century paintings of Arcimboldo, are masterpieces of the genre.

Morue
Sole
168
Saumon
59
Rascasse
59
Colinot
79
Bar
128
Lotte
149
Carrelet
39
Rouget Barbet

SORRY WE HAVE SOLD
OUT OF CRABS AT THE

At Richard & Julie's shop in Wells-next-the-Sea in Norfolk, Rose sells seafood fished by the Davis family. Pictures of family members, in their roles as both fishermen and lifeboat men, deck the walls, along with

a hearty display of fishing nets and giant plastic shellfish and crustaceans. Here the conversation is as salty as the specialities on sale. *Above*: a giant albino lobster, caught by Mr Davis senior in 1970.

HUTS & CABINS

Whatever the name their owners give them – *crampottes* at Biarritz, *caloges* in Normandy and *rorbus* in Norway – fishermen's huts, whether on stilts, carved out of the cliff or simply standing on the shore, always overlook the sea. Lining a river estuary or standing at the entrance to a harbour, they wait for the fleet to return and land its catch. Impregnated with their own strong perfume, a heady blend of brine, pitch and petrol, these are places of secrets and reveries. They are workplaces, so sleeping in them is forbidden. This is where the fisherman stores his gear – engines, oars, lobster pots, nets, buoys, ropes and paint pots; this is the workshop where he washes, scrapes, sorts, grades and packs shellfish and crustaceans; this sometimes even doubles as his shop, where he sells his catch only a few yards from his boat.

Near Felixstowe in Suffolk, in a hut built on stilts straddling the River Deben, a fisherman wearing a canvas smock which has been artistically patched, cleans and sells the sole, plaice and mackerel that he has just caught. Sometimes in the summer, fishermen's huts are transformed into restaurants, as at New Harbor and Stonington on the coast of Maine in the United States, where clam chowder is served in paper cups, and even boiled lobsters are to be had. These huts, many of which are given beguiling names such as 'Sorceress', 'Zulu' or simply 'Judy', represent the fisherman's refuge, the only place where he can be alone, and they are cherished almost as much as the boats to which they form the 'annex'.

On the old harbour at Biarritz, Monsieur Lecuona's *crampotte* bears a Basque name, *Batxe-Satxe* (Softly Softly), like its neighbours *Ixilix* and *Ttuku-Tukku*. The fishermen who rent them from the local council amuse themselves by looking on them as

NEW ZEALAND
Apples

CRESSIDA

Page 51: the inside of an English fisherman's hut, used for storing gear and cleaning fish. Despite their functional nature, fishermen's huts – part toy box, part treasure chest – have their own special allure. *These pages*: when fishermen repaint their boats in spring, they use the doors of their huts as palettes to try out different colours.

a 'little independent republic'. Bad weather often keeps them inside, forcing them to wait for better conditions before setting off in pursuit of sea bream or cuttlefish; this is where they sit, enjoying a bite to eat while they 'wait and see'. It is rare, nevertheless, to find fishermen's huts in the centre of a town or village. Usually they stand in isolated places, in a no man's land of sand and sea, on an empty peninsula or a windswept estuary. Looking out to distant horizons, they underline the vast immensities of the seascape in the same way as a tiny red sail on a yacht far out to sea.

These huts are inextricably linked with the spaces in which they are built. In Maine, for example, they form an integral part of the landscape – a tangled labyrinth of islands and peninsulas, covered with pine forests petering out on the rocks that are as round and gleaming as the numerous seals in this region. Built of shingles, the huts stand on the silvery-grey landing stages where the lobster boats unload the day's catch. The Norwegian *rorbus*, raised on stilts and nearly always painted red, first appeared in the nineteenth century on the Lofoten Islands, an archipelago stretching like a great wall of mountains standing in the sea, 168 kilometres (104 miles) into the Arctic Circle. The inhabitants of the Lofoten Islands still earn their living by fishing cod. Called *skrei* in Norwegian, meaning 'the jumpy one', the cod set out from the Barents Sea, north of Norway, in December, making for their spawning grounds in Vestfjord, the immense fjord that separates the archipelago from the Norwegian coast, and the fish remain there until April every year. After the cod-fishing season, the *rorbus* are often rented out to summer visitors.

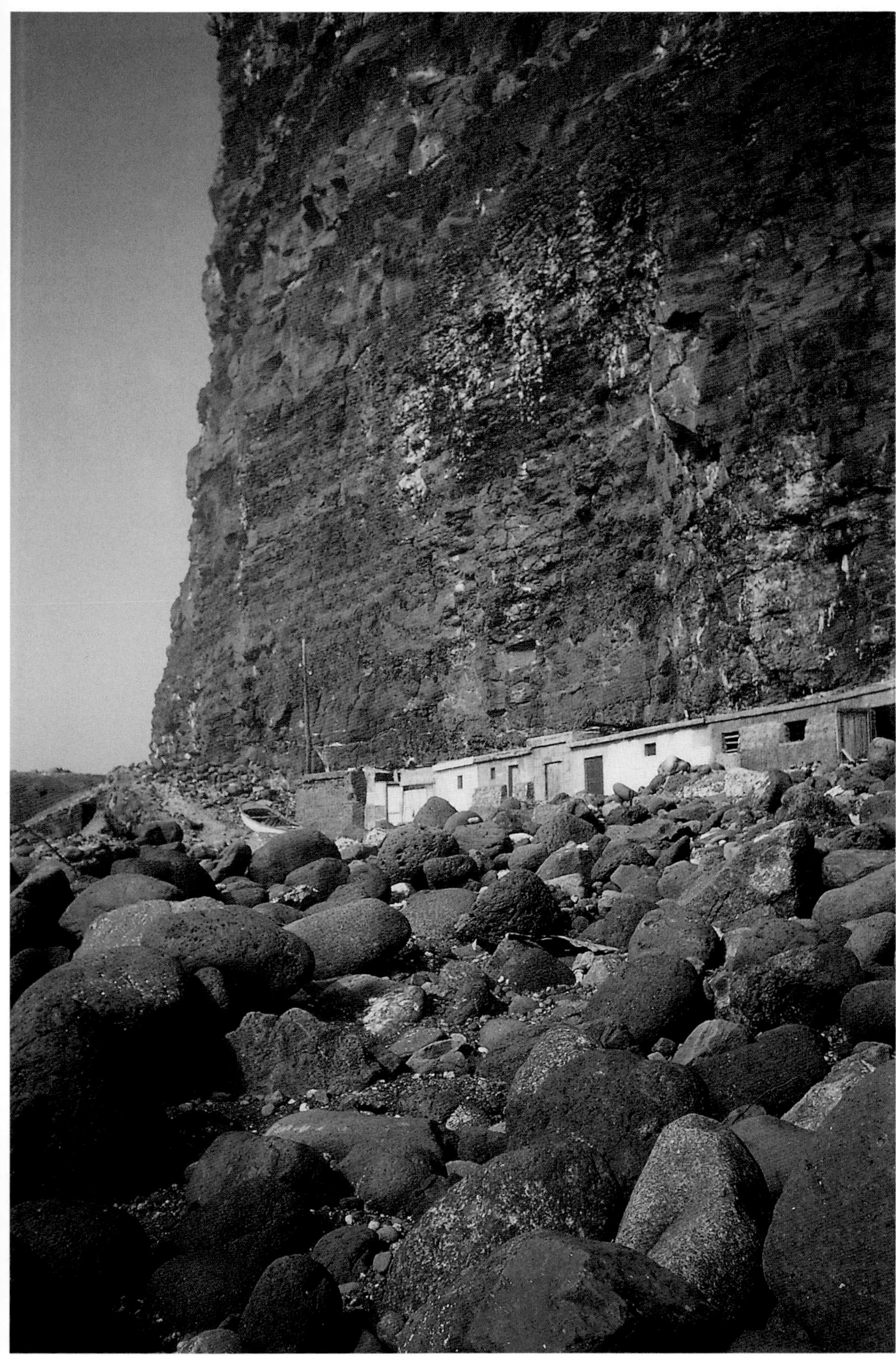

Opposite: a row of wooden fishermen's huts, blackened with pitch, on the Blyth estuary at Southwold in Suffolk.
Left: looking out towards America, breezeblock huts huddle under a volcanic cliff at La Palma in the Canaries.
Following pages: summer cabins on the Ile aux Marins, south of the islands of Saint-Pierre and Miquelon, 25 kilometres (15 miles) off the coast of Newfoundland.

Above and opposite above: a lobster fisherman's hut at Stonington, state of Maine. Bright yellow buoys, sea-coloured lobster pots, a woodpile and model boats make up its eclectic interior décor.

Opposite below: a hut in a Lowestoft shipyard, Suffolk. *Below*: entrance to a *crampotte* in Biarritz, south-west France. The pennants attached to floats in the foreground are used to mark the places where lobster pots have been dropped into the sea.

MN
720-
260 S

H BENARD
TEL. 46_85 2621

Preceding pages: the hut belonging to Monsieur Sonnette, an oyster farmer of Marennes, near Rochefort, Charente-Maritime.
Right: the inside of the same hut. On the bench, the oysters are scraped, cleaned and sorted according to size, before being placed in *bourriches*, or baskets. An open fire, lit until Easter, helps to ward off the damp.

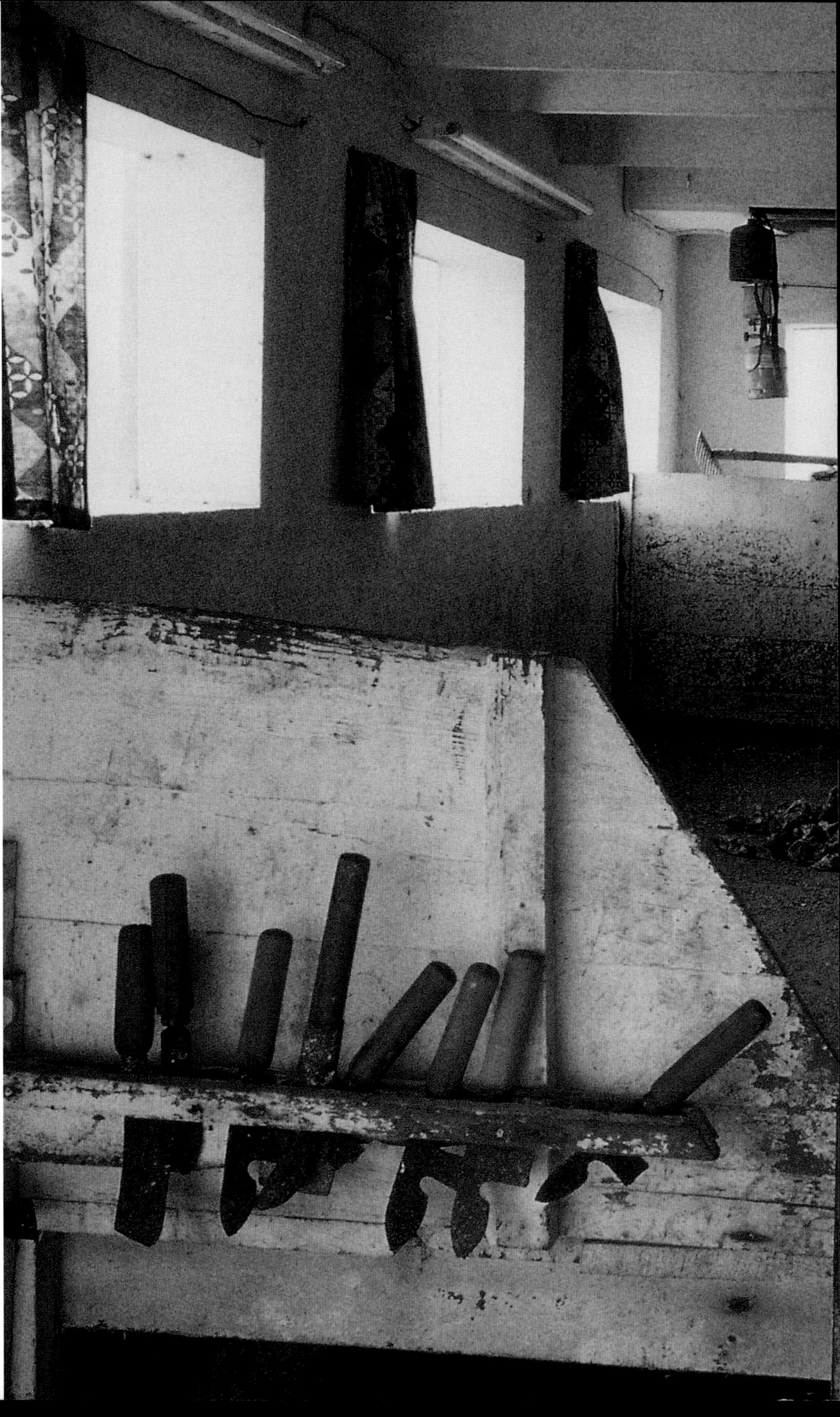

Below: a cabin beside a lobster pool in Maine creates an image reminiscent of the paintings of Andrew Wyeth or the photographs of Eliot Porter.

Bottom: Drift Wood Cottage, a pink and blue cabin at the end of a landing stage on the Outer Banks, a group of islands stretching 100 kilometres (60 miles) down the coast of North Carolina.

Right: salt cod hung to dry outside a pair of *rorbus,* a typical feature of the Lofoten Islands in Norway. Generally painted red, these cabins are used by cod fishermen from February to April, and in the summer are often rented out to tourists.

A hut made out of the hull of a fishing lugger, now at the Fishermen's Museum in Hastings. This Sussex fishing town has no true harbour: the fishing fleet is simply dragged up the stony beach by winch or tractor, and for this reason boats are allowed a maximum length of ten metres (33 feet). When taken out of service, the light and manoeuvrable luggers were often turned into workshops.

Opposite: Hastings in the early 20th century. The linen, hemp or cotton nets rotted if left damp, so they were hung to dry in wooden 'net shops' on the beach, at the foot of the cliffs overlooking the Channel. As the land the shops stood on was subject to heavy taxes, the fishermen decided to build upwards.

Above: these curious vertical structures can still be seen at the Hastings Fishermen's Museum, established on a voluntary basis in 1956. The museum's reconstruction of the old fishing buildings manages to combine historical accuracy with picturesque charm.

Most fishing in the Atlantic, the Channel and the North Sea today is done with nets or lobster pots. For many years, nets were made from hemp, cotton, horsehair or even sisal. To increase their resistance to damp and salt, they were treated with pitch or sometimes acacia bark imported from India. These days, nets are made of synthetic fibres and are more resistant. The fisherman chooses his colour with care, matching it to the local waters in order to trick the fish. There are all kinds of nets, generally bought in 'layers' of varying thickness. The size of the mesh is crucial and strictly regulated: the net functions as a giant sieve, and its mesh is calculated to catch only the targeted fish above a certain size. Nets – whether trawl, gill or drift – are adapted to a wide variety of fishing techniques. Since 1950, the most common of these is trawling, an increasingly efficient method and also the most controversial

NETS & POTS

on ecological grounds. The funnel-shaped trawl net, suspended from the stern of the trawler, seems like an enormous maw that gulps down everything in its path, while the trawlers themselves, equipped with ever more powerful engines, are moving at faster and faster speeds. This highly unselective technique (over a third of the catch is tossed back into the sea) is partly responsible for the depletion of fish stocks in the waters of the Continental Shelf. Fish are currently the victims of a silent massacre which threatens perilously to undermine the balance of marine ecosystems, while global warming which is heating up the sea, pollution and the disappearance of plankton pose a significant danger to many marine species.

Nets, though fatal to the fish that are ensnared in them, are nevertheless fragile affairs, even when made from today's synthetic fibres, and they need frequent

Preceding page: lobster pots, Brittany.
Right: nets swallow everything in their path, including the crustaceans which, as here, get tangled up in them. This spectacularly draped net in West Bay, Dorset looks like some baroque stage curtain.

These pages: collecting mussels at Brancaster in Norfolk. Mussels form natural clusters on rocks, but are also farmed in mussel beds or on ropes stretched underwater. They are still sometimes sorted, rinsed and graded for size on the shore in traditional machines that look like some strange giant insect, before being bundled up in bags of orange or purple mesh: the only splashes of colour in a monochrome seascape of silt and sand, rimmed by pale dunes.

mending – a delicate and painstaking operation rather like both knitting and lace-making. Armed with needle and shuttle, fishermen are constantly restitching, tying, edging and patching. Sometimes, they claim, the holes are caused by beluga whales, mythical 'monsters' of the deep related to dolphins, which rip through the nets to devour the catch under the fishermen's noses.

Apart from the trawl nets, the 'fishing-machines', fishermen also use 'sleeping' techniques, such as hoop nets and pots for catching lobsters, crabs and crayfish. Traditionally hemispherical in form and made of willow, most of these traps are now cylindrical in shape and made of metal, of chestnut laths bound together with nets dipped in pitch, or of synthetic materials. The entrance to the pot, positioned at the end of the cylinder or along the side, is funnel-shaped, so that the crustaceans, attracted by the bait, can creep inside but cannot get out again. These utterly functional objects also provide a decorative leitmotif in the landscape of the fishing port. Even when they have been abandoned along the shore, they are imprinted – for those who know how to look – with the poetry of the everyday. A number of museums that have sprung up along the coasts of France, Britain and North America have realized the importance of these objects, and devise displays that allow the public to enter into the world of fishing. One of the most intriguing, perhaps, is housed in the small disused lighthouse at Pemaquid Point on the coast of Maine in the United States. Unsophisticated and touching, and completely removed from the pompous atmosphere of most maritime museums, it has been created with great humanity by a handful of fishermen's wives. They began it all with just a couple of nets, a willow lobster pot and a clutch of buoys painted in a fishing family's own distinctive colours.

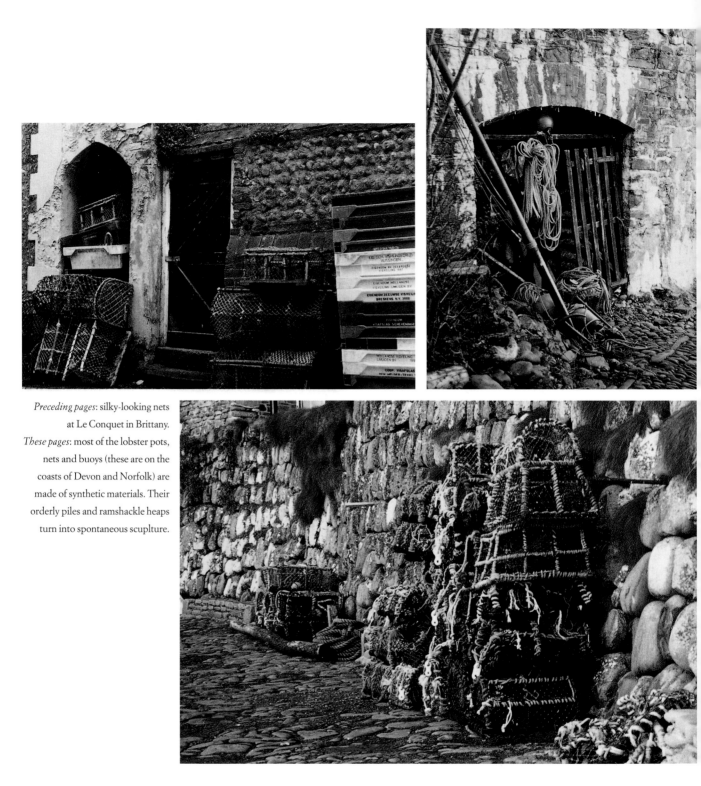

Preceding pages: silky-looking nets at Le Conquet in Brittany. *These pages*: most of the lobster pots, nets and buoys (these are on the coasts of Devon and Norfolk) are made of synthetic materials. Their orderly piles and ramshackle heaps turn into spontaneous scuplture.

Below right: in the wake of Mathurin Méheut (1882–1958), the great Breton painter of the interwar years, many artists have caught the rough beauty of fishing gear. Some retired fishermen never tire of painting the lighthouses and boats that have formed the unchanging backdrop of their lives.

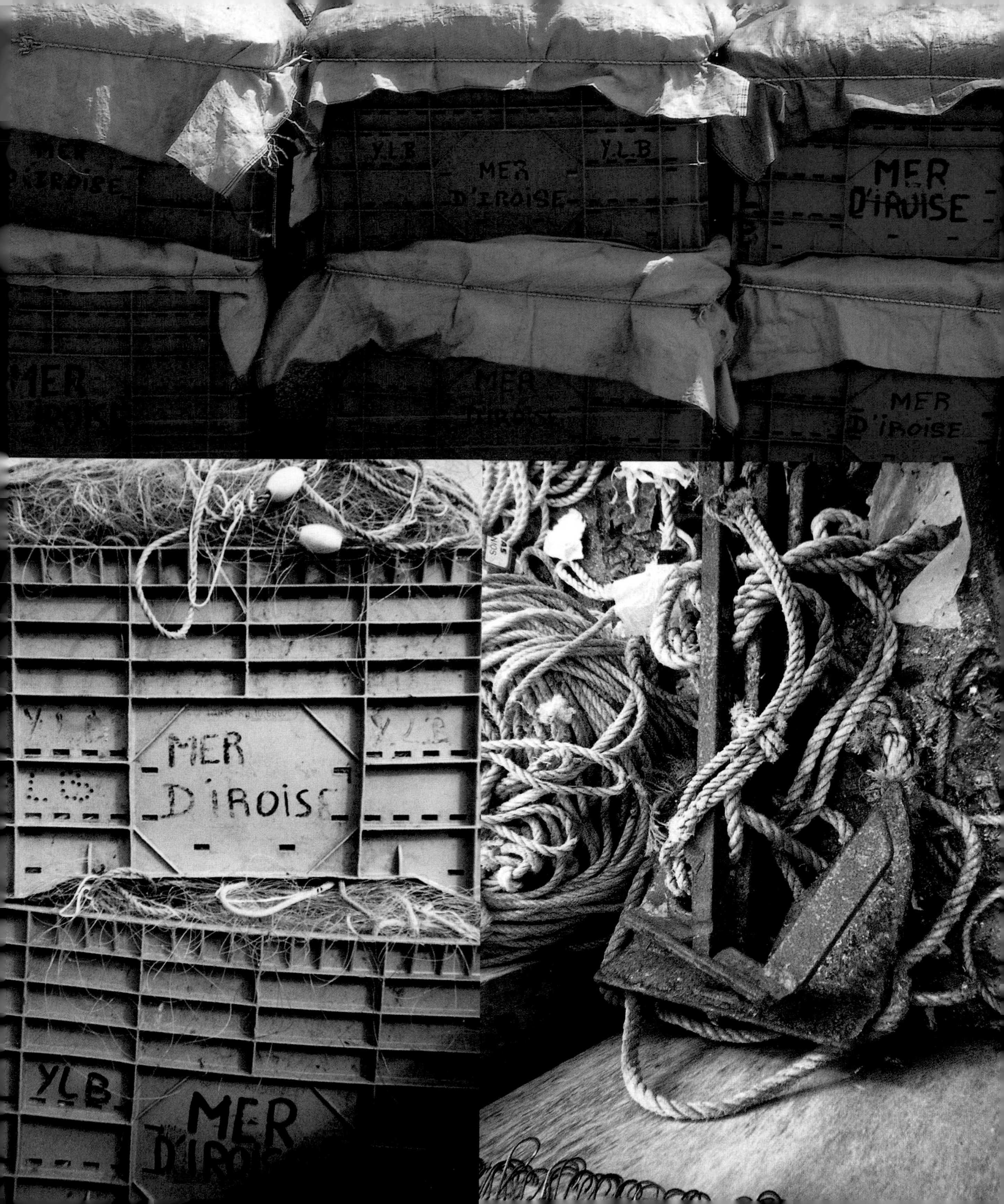

YLB
MER D'IROISE
YLB
MER D'IROISE
MER D'IROISE
YLB
MER D'IROISE
YLB
MER

Previous pages : ropes, grapnels, lobster pots, buoys, hooks, pennants, anchors and floats. *Below and opposite*: in the little disused lighthouse at Pemaquid Point, on the coast of Maine, built in the 19th century, a group of fishermen's wives have set up a

museum in honour of the everyday objects of a fishing community. Fishing nets, marker buoys, nautical maps, lifebuoys and brightly coloured lobster pots are all shown side by side like so many souvenirs, with all the unsophisticated charm of a family photo album.

Tourist became victim of the sea
NEW ENGLAND SINK GILL NET

BACK ON

TERRA FIRMA

Preceding pages: no boats will put out to sea today from Ile Molène, lost in the Breton mist.

These pages: Finisterrae, the house of François Morin *(below)* at Lampaul on the Ile d'Ouessant in Brittany, is still home to his daughter Violette. In the 1930s, this famous

lifeboat man decorated his entire house, helped by his brother-in-law, a former seaman who turned to cabinet-making after an accident at sea. A few model ships have been added over the years, along with a barometer and a giant lobster found in the Baie du Stiff in 1950.

‘My home is my boat,’ states a fisherman. When they are young and spend half their lives at sea, mariners do indeed make it a point of honour to maintain their boats with every possible care. They paint them and repaint them, titivating them lovingly. Only accident, illness or retirement can take them away from the sea and condemn them to live on land, and this they experience as an exile and as a loss. ‘The sea is my whole life,’ explains a fifty-four-year-old Breton. ‘I only feel right on the water. You have to have seen the sea at night, the immensity of the sky and stars, to understand.’

While a fisherman is still working, the house is the exclusive domain of his wife. She strives as best she can to make it conform to modern ideas of comfort. The less it differs from those of her neighbours the better. Convention is all. Fishermen do not like to be reminded of the time when their parents and grandparents were as impoverished as the miners and factory workers – when some of them were even forced to live in conditions of squalor in the converted hulls of abandoned boats. Above all, the house must not remind them of the homes of the past, which to today’s fishermen seem poverty-stricken and lacking in comfort.

Left and opposite: in a hut in the garden, Violette has created a sort of mausoleum around the lifebuoy from her father’s last boat. This presides over an assortment of whelk and giant ormer or abalone shells, ‘unusual’ pebbles, floats and ‘anything else I can’t bring myself to throw away’.

Monsieur Renouf’s place at Cap de la Hague, near Cherbourg, was a typical example. It was extremely dark, and imbued with an indefinable smell combining damp, pitch, brine and rubber boots. Monsieur Renouf, a war orphan who died in the 1980s, loved it regardless, undeterred by its earth floor and its evident lack of the most basic comforts. A fisherman and volunteer lifeboat man, very much his own person, he had made this his lair, a refuge that defied classification and that reflected his own strong personality. Here he amassed, in great disorder, objects connected with his everyday life and his passion for the sea. This totally individual approach is fast disappearing

VIOLE
LA BRISE
BREST
ROYAL

*W*hen boats were taken out of service in the early 20th century, it was not unusual on both sides of the Channel to beach them, patch them up and improvise a rudimentary roof out of tarpaulins covered with wooden laths or pitch to serve as dwellings for the poorest fishermen in the community.

Chaputzot et Truffart,

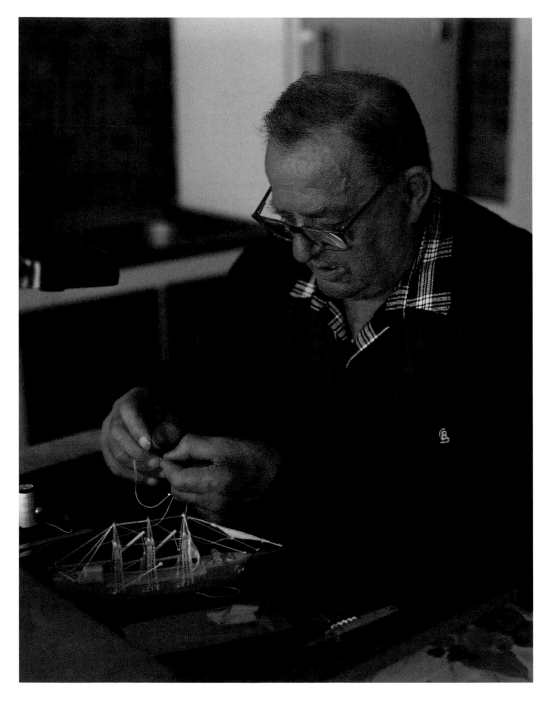

Left: in his youth, Monsieur Auzoux, a native of Sassetot-le-Mauconduit near Fécamp, was ship's boy on a *terre-neuvas*, or Newfoundland fishing boat, and so he experienced the final years of those great cod-fishing expeditions. Now he nostalgically makes ships' models from the great age of sail.

Opposite: Monsieur Renouf spent his entire life on the Cotentin peninsula in Normandy, where he fished for crab and lobster and was a famously courageous member of the local lifeboat crew. He started every day with *un petit calva* (a tot of Calvados), and was never known to wash his only plate – over the years it acquired an impressive accretion of 'sedimentary layers'.

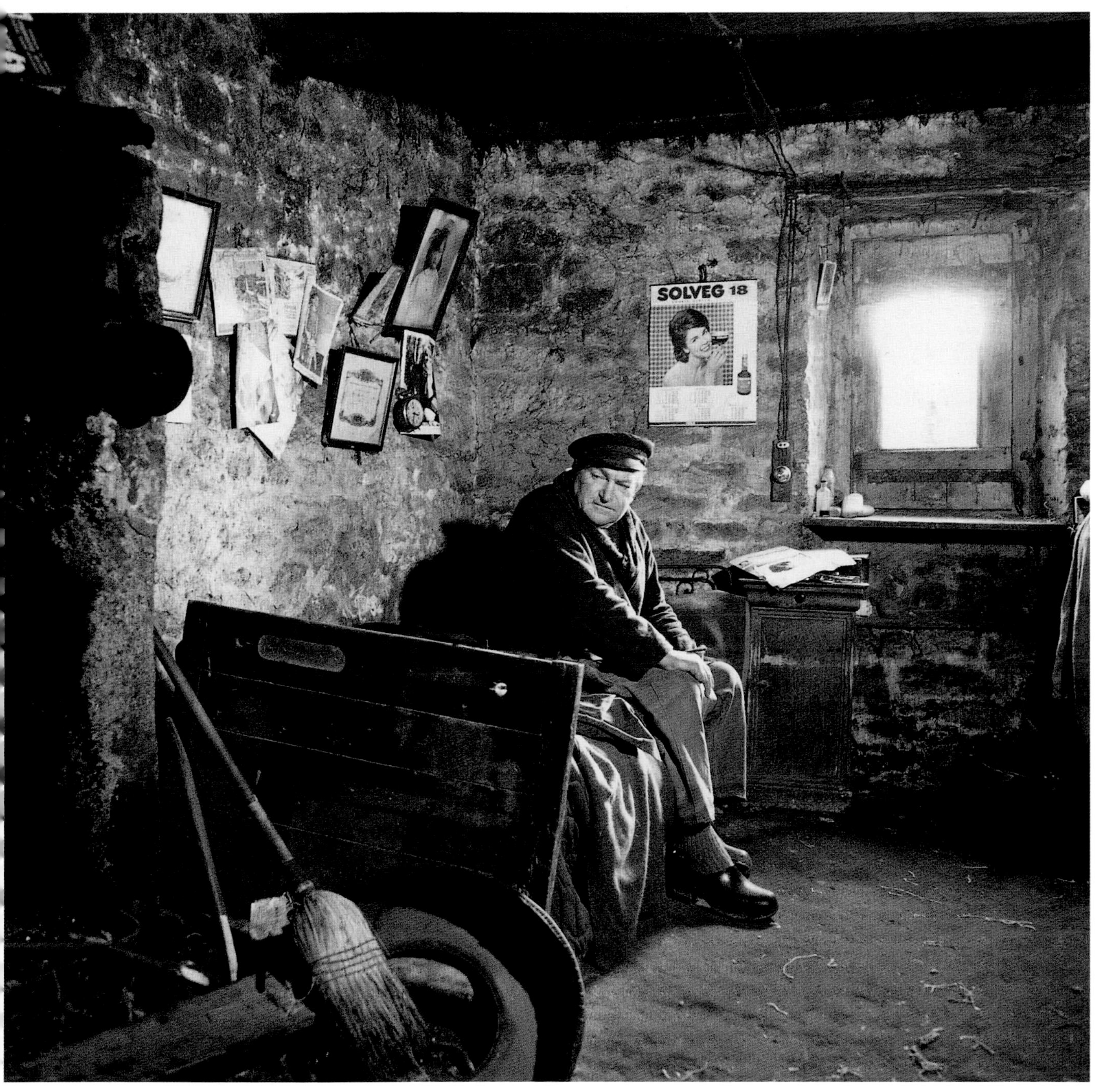
SOLVEG 18

today in an age when decoration is subordinate to functionalism. And yet, when fishermen stop working they sometimes view with a certain nostalgia objects connected with their former way of life, tough and relentless though it might have been. Some start making model ships, working in the garage or on a corner of the table. Others are more original, abandoning the idea that a house should be anonymous, and filling their homes with souvenirs and ornaments all linked with the world of the sea. François Morin, well-known fisherman and lifeboat man, decorated his whole house in Finistère with the help of his brother-in-law, a former seaman turned cabinet-maker, who made the dark and elaborate Renaissance-style furniture, while he himself took care of the decorative scheme. The walls have disappeared under souvenirs, the pride of the collection a lobster of such impressive size – it must have been at least a hundred years old when caught – that Monsieur Morin forbade his family to eat it, determined as he was to preserve it. He put the 'monster' on an ant heap and let the ants strip the carapace bare.

These pages: a French postcard from the end of the 19th century shows an upturned fishing boat used as a little house. However charming it looks, it is an indication of the desperate need and poverty in the old fishing communities.

Sam and Beryl Kerrison, who live near Cromer in Norfolk, have made a garden around their house that is as delightful as it is extravagant. Sam was a herring fisherman all his working life, while Beryl caught shrimps. Now, every morning, winter and summer, she walks along the beach with the dog, on the look-out for finds which she and her husband will later assemble, transform, paint and arrange according to their whim. Their astonishing garden, somewhere between Derek Jarman's at Dungeness and that of Le Facteur Cheval near Lyons, quivers, whistles and echoes with the strange sounds produced by the many weather vanes, windmills, flags and birds made of wood or plastic, that surround their house, set off by the wind which blows strongly here the whole day long. Beryl's finds are mostly pennants, floats and cork buoys, but once she actually found a mammoth's tooth. Paul Townsend, originally

POSTES
FRANÇAISE
POSTES

Left: in an old seaman's house on the Ile d'Ouessant in Brittany, Paul Townsend runs an antique shop that pays tribute to the world of the sea.
Opposite: another islander has painted his entire house in blue. The interior of this house is constructed throughout from wood salvaged from shipwrecks – once a common solution to the problem of finding materials on this isolated island, 20 km (12 miles) off the coast of northern Finistère, and a practical one too, given the number of ships that used to founder on the surrounding rocks each year.

from Liverpool, and now living on the Ile d'Ouessant off Brittany, collects objects from the past. A Sunday fisherman, he spends the rest of his week selling antiques. His collection, though undeniably more sophisticated than Beryl Kerrison's finds, nonetheless expresses the same love of the sea and of the things traditionally connected with it. From Wales to Finistère, he searches the French and British coasts for souvenirs of the sea, furniture and ornaments, which he displays beside his large collection of naive paintings by old fishermen, who seem never to tire of depicting the lighthouses and boats that have been a constant feature of their daily lives.

Yet, however interested a fisherman may be in his house, he never strays far from the path to the café or the pub. Up until the 1960s, fishermen's cafés in France were distinguished by their wholeheartedly kitsch and exuberant decorative schemes, featuring fishing nets, faded old photographs of fishermen and trawlers, flares, the shells of lobsters, crayfish and crabs, fragments of wrecked boats and starfish, hung everywhere all over on the walls. Then this taste for excess gradually went out of fashion. The stripped-down look is now the thing – basic colours of blue and white, possibly with touches of polished mahogany, the only concession to fantasy being the occasional copper porthole.

Opposite: *Au Soleil Levant* (At the Rising Sun), a fishermen's bar on the harbour at Granville, Normandy. *Following pages*: the Sailors' Reading Room, established in 1869 at Southwold in Suffolk. Fishermen still come here to read the newspaper, play cards or chat. The walls are covered with model ships in bottles, ships' figureheads and portraits of 'old sea dogs'.

From the beginning of the twentieth century until the 1960s, fishermen were also regular visitors to *abris du marin* or seamen's missions. These acted as social centres, dispensaries, studios, workshops and libraries, supported by benefactors who were partly paternalistic and partly forerunners of the social services and welfare state. Their principal *raison d'être* was to inculcate the fishermen with an intellectual, moral and religious education, in this way ensuring (it was earnestly hoped) that they would become less frequent visitors to the bar on the corner.

CONFIANCE
JOKER
PÔULBOT
CARPE DIEM
CONFIANCE

Donations

At Eccles in Norfolk, Sam and Beryl Kerrison have created a remarkable garden, as noisy as it is colourful, and quite as eccentric as those of Derek Jarman at Dungeness and Le Facteur Cheval near Lyons. Lying beside the road against a backdrop of sand dunes, it is a forest of sheds, buoys, masts and rigging, on which these two retired fishing people hang their daily offerings of whistling weathervanes and all manner of found objects.

Although the business of fishing may have changed beyond all recognition, and, moreover, is in serious decline, many traditional customs – gloomy or joyful, simple or lyrical, but invariably touching – continue to be observed today. The sea has always been celebrated with great feasts and festivals. Beyond the simple pleasures of care-free fun, these were intended as an exorcism of the danger that was a constant presence for seafarers at the mercy of the sea. Over two hundred disappear into the sea each year off the coasts of France, Britain and Spain. Neither courage nor experience can guarantee survival. 'The sea is always the stronger,' observes a seaman.

While it brings about a heightened awareness of life for the men who go out in fishing boats, this daily exposure to the dangers of the sea also accounts for the survival of a whole range of traditions intended to ward off danger. Just before the annual

RITES & RITUALS

departure of the fishing fleet to catch cod in the waters off Newfoundland, Dunkirk was the scene of a great Mardi Gras carnival – a tradition that survives to this day, even though the conditions of the fishermen's lives have changed. During the two months of carnival the atmosphere was full of craziness and excess: the participants were armed with multicoloured umbrellas and wore masks and improbable fancy dress. The streets almost literally exploded with the arrival of the *Visschersbende* ('band of fishermen' in Flemish), for, as the cavalcade passed by, tradition required that the mayor, standing on the balcony of the hôtel de ville, should hurl kippers into the crowd. Each year, the inhabitants of Dunkirk were bombarded with no less than five hundred kilos (a thousand pounds) of fish. The custom has become so popular in northern France, indeed, that it has been responsible for reviving a number of

A legacy of the days when the fishing fleets set off to spend long months fishing for cod in the waters off Iceland and Newfoundland, festival of the sea still follow one another along France's coasts. This is especially so in the north around Dunkirk, where the tradition remains particularly strong.

Page 105 and above: *fête de la mer* at Audresselles, near Dunkirk. *Opposite above*: blessing a *flobard* at Audresselles. *Left*: *fête de la mer* at Dunkirk, complete with traditional jewelry, lace and headgear. *Opposite below*: launch of a fishing boat at Etaples in the Pas-de-Calais, 1908.

smokeries, where the herring are smoked over beech sawdust. Around 15 August each year, seaports on all of France's coasts mark the Feast of the Assumption of the Virgin with many variations on the traditional festivals of the sea, including celebrations in honour of fish, crabs and sardines. At Saint-Jean-de-Luz in south-west France there is even a *nuit du thon*, a night dedicated to tuna.

All these celebrations mingle the sacred and the profane. A morning Mass is generally followed by processions that wind down to the harbour. Carried by the men, multicoloured banners, miraculous statues of the Virgin and ex-votos that sleep for the rest of the year in the darkness of some chapel are paraded through the streets. Sometimes the procession is followed by a fishing display or cooking demonstration, with tips on how to fillet fish, slice tuna into steaks and scald seaweed. This is not an occasion for fancy dress, but the women wear their traditional headdress and jewelry, while the parish priest ventures to the far end of the jetty, or even out to sea in a boat, in order to bless the sea and toss it offerings of bouquets and floral chaplets. In Boulogne, festivities are intensified on the day when the black Virgin, said to have

arrived mysteriously in the town one night in the seventh century, is illuminated and paraded forth. To mark the occasion, the women wear their lace bonnets, called 'suns' because they are in the shape of the sun, and their special gold earrings, called *dorlots*. When a sailor is in danger at sea, he prays to the Virgin, promising her an ex-voto if he is saved: perhaps a model of the boat menaced by waves, a marble plaque engraved in gold, or a colour photograph. The most appealing ex-votos are those naive paintings that recount in detail, like a comic strip, all the ordeals undergone.

And now the shipping forecast. '…There are warnings of gales, in Viking, Forties, Rockall…Fisher, North German Bight, Humber south-east veering south-west 6 to gale force 8 south. Moderate, occasionally poor….' The litany of warnings now available to shipping is itself a little marvel, yet still disaster strikes. Mourning, too, has its rituals. This evening the *Perle de Jade* (the Jade Pearl) is lost with its crew of twenty, all men from Lorient, Finistère. Last month it was the *Marcel-Adrien*, with eight men of different nationalities. As one fisherman's wife said, 'Only the sea will ever know what happened.

Below and following pages: *fête de la Mer* at Grand-Fort-Philippe, near Dunkirk. The route of the procession is decided by the lifeboat committee, and those who live along it decorate their houses with flowers and fishing nets in honour of the Virgins and ex-votos that will be paraded through the streets.

VENDRE
GRAVELINES
OPTEX
32

42

When the men go aboard we try to convince ourselves that no harm will come to them.' The seamen's chaplain at Saint-Jean-de-Luz adds, 'I was a fisherman before I became a priest, and I know what I'm talking about. The families of these men need ceremonies to help them mourn, to help them face up to reality.'

At Sainte-Adresse, near Le Havre, the mother of a young seaman lost at sea in the nineteenth century commissioned a life-size sculpture of her son for the cliff-top chapel of Notre-Dame des Flots. Beside the chapel stands a curious and rather phallic monument erected by a grieving wife to her lost husband, which now serves as a landmark for sailors, like a lighthouse in the mist. Until the 1960s, the Ile d'Ouessant, scene of countless shipwrecks down the centuries, held funeral rites for drowned seamen whose bodies were never recovered. Known as the *Proëlla*, from a Breton word meaning 'bringing home', this extremely rare ceremony was probably of pagan origins and was a symbolic burial, with the drowned man represented by a little wax cross. The ritual began with a night's vigil at the dead man's house, and the next day the whole community went to lay the little cross in the cemetery, in a tiny chapel built specifically for this purpose. According to tradition, mariners must be buried, otherwise they will be condemned to wander the world, forever seeking eternal rest. In the seamen's chapels, built high on cliff-tops like signals of hope, hardly a day goes by even now without someone coming in to light a candle, to lay down some flowers, or to write a grateful message to the Virgin or a request for a loved one, dead or living, in the spiral-bound notebooks under the statues of Notre-Dame du Bon Voyage, Notre-Dame de Grâce, St Rita (patron saint of lost causes) or Notre-Dame du Bon Retour.

Below: Notre-Dame de Grâce, a little seamen's chapel near Honfleur, Normandy, is filled with ex-votos, naive paintings and model ships hung from the ceiling, all offered to the Virgin by grateful seamen 'saved' from shipwrecks. The ceiling, painted blue,

is in the form of an inverted ship's hull, and the walls are completely covered by hundreds of marble plaques, on which the faithful have had engraved in gold the words '*merci*' and '*reconnaissance*'. *Opposite*: the imposing church of Saint-Vincent at Ciboure on the south-west Atlantic coast of France, built in the 16th century.

Above left: the chapel of Sainte-Adresse in Normandy contains the life-size statue of J. H. Silvera, drowned at sea in 1857, aged just twenty.
Below left, below and opposite: Notre-Dame des Flots at Le Havre. Beneath the photograph of the *Ginette le Borgne* are listed the

names of all the hands — sailors, ship's boys, mechanics, 'salters' and 'slicers' — who went down with her in 1951. Against an astonishing Gothic Revival background, model ships, artificial flowers, statues and portraits drift in heaps, deposited like geological strata since the age of the great cod-fishing expeditions.

MERCI
1966-198
SOUVE
KE
6.7.94
M R I

A MON MARI
A MON MARI
En mémoire
de Charles MOREAU,
âgé de 19 ans dé-
cédé le 26
mars 1897.
Priez Dieu pour lui.
182
MŒURS ET COUTUMES B
NALEC (Côtes-du-Nord). — Le Cimeti

NES
Mur des Disparus en Mer.

Brittany, where the traditional cult of the dead remains strong, still has its *Murs des Disparus*, or 'Walls for those Lost at Sea', where relatives of drowned seamen come to meditate and pray. *Left*: the *Mur des Disparus* at Ploubazlanec, near Paimpol, Brittany, pays tribute to the memory of the two thousand seamen lost at sea during the great Icelandic fishing expeditions undertaken by local

fleets from 1852 until 1959. Here a woman in mourning kneels before the commemorative plaques, beaded wreaths and lace made from nautical twine that were in vogue in the early 20th century. *Above*: a melancholy memorial, which looks as if it could have come from a kitsch photograph by artists Pierre et Gilles, in the parish church of Winterton-on-Sea on the Norfolk coast.

ACKNOWLEDGMENTS

Special thanks from the author to Mike Tighe, Ivan Terestchenko, Min Hogg, Jacques Dirand and Samuel Dhote. The author would also like to thank Héloïse Wirth, Laeticia Yhap, Michael Rycroft, Martine Denisot, Jean-Paul Colin, Paul Townsend, Violette Morin, Jacqueline and Philippe Giacolette, Ramuncho de Saint-Amand, Elfreda Pownall, Daniel Allisy, Nicolas Gilles, Monsieur Lecuona, Wendy Booth and Lesley Howard, Serge Lucas, Rupert Thomas, Barbara Huppé, Vincent Knapp, Didier and Valérie Guegan, Françoise Teynac, François Dautresme, Jacqueline Prodom (Ifremer), Sophie Hérolt

PHOTOGRAPHIC CREDITS

(a = above, b = below, c = centre, l = left, r = right)

Photo Damian Bird: 24br, 44al, 45a, 72–73 **Photo Marie-France Boyer**: 3, 7r, 10–11, 18ar, 18bl, 19ar, 19c, 41a, 43, 45br, 55, 58a, 59a, 64a, 68a, 68b, 76bl, 80al, 81bl, 81br, 99, 114, endpapers **Photo M. R. Carter**: 64b **Contact Press Images, Paris**: 15 (Photo Giorgia Fiorio) **Photo François Dautresme**: 93 **Photo Samuel Dhote**: 18al, 18c, 18br, 19 al, 19bl, 19br, 80b, 105, 106l, 106r, 107h, 107b, 108-109, 110-111h, 110-111b, 112-113 **Photo Jacques Dirand**: 13, 44b, 59b, 97, 115, 116al, 116cr **Photo Min Hogg**: 4–5, 8al, 8ar, 8b, 9, 24ar, 24bl, 31a, 31bl, 31br, 51, 53, 54, 58b, 80ar, endpapers **© Judges Postcards Ltd., Hastings, www. judges.co.uk**: 68–69 **Photo Eric Morin**: 35, 44ar, 60–61, 62–63 **Photo © Musée des Terre-Neuvas, Fécamp**: 23 **Photo Courtesy the Norfolk Museums & Archaeology Service**: 32 **Sea and See, Paris**: 7l (© M. C. Nguyen), 7cr (Collection Caziel), 17 (© A. Fyot), 20, 24al (© Daniel Allisy), 25 (© M. C. Nguyen), 26 (Collection Caziel), 26–27 (Collection Caziel), 28–29 (© Serge Lucas), 36 (Collection Caziel), 36–37 (Collection Caziel), 38–39 (© Serge Lucas), 42–43 (© Eric Lorang), 56–57 (© Serge Lucas), 64–65 (© Serge Lucas), 66–67 (© Daniel Allisy), 90–91 (Collection Caziel), 94–95 (Collection Caziel), 118–119 (Collection Caziel) **Photo Ivan Terestchenko**: 1, 2, 7c, 45bl, 46, 47, 71, 76al, 76ar, 76br, 77, 79bl, 79br, 81a, 84–85, 86l, 86r, 87l, 87r, 88, 89, 92l, 92ar, 92br, 96al, 96 ar, 96bl, 96br, 116b, 117 **Photo Mike Tighe**: 7cl, 21, 41b, 48–49, 49, 52, 74a, 74b, 75, 78al, 78ar, 78b, 79a, 102, 103a, 103b, 103cr, 119, endpapers **True's Yard Collection, King's Lynn**: 6, 33 **The World of Interiors**: 82a (Photo Ivan Terestchenko), 82b (Photo Ivan Terestchenko), 82–83 (Photo Ivan Terestchenko), 100–101 (Photo Peter Baistow)

MUSEUMS TO VISIT

FRANCE

Musée des terre-neuvas et de la pêche, 27 boulevard Albert 1er, 76 400 Fécamp. Tel. +33-(0)2 35 28 31 99 **Musée de la mer**, Plateau de l'Atalaye, 64 202 Biarritz. Tel. +33-(0)5 59 22 33 34 **Musée de la pêche**, 3 rue Vauban (Ville Close), 29 181 Concarneau. Tel. +33-(0)2 98 97 10 20 **Musée du bateau (Port-Musée)**, place de l'Enfer, 29 100 Douarnenez. Tel. +33-(0)2 98 92 65 20

ENGLAND

Hastings Fishermen's Museum, Rock-a-Nore Road, Hastings, East Sussex, TN34 3DW. Tel. +44-(0)1424 461 446 **Maritime Museum**, Sparrows Nest, Whapload Road, Lowestoft, Suffolk, NR32 1XG. Tel. +44-(0)1502 561 963 **Cromer Museum**, Tucker Street, Cromer, Norfolk, NR27 9HB. Tel. +44-(0)1263 513 543 **True's Yard Fishing Museum**, North Street, King's Lynn, Norfolk, PE30 1QW. Tel. +44-(0)1553 770 479 **Southwold Museum,** 9–11 Victoria Street, Southwold, Suffolk, IP18 6HZ. Tel. +44-(0)1502 72 33 74

UNITED STATES OF AMERICA

The Fishermen's Museum, Pemaquid Point Road, New Harbor, ME 04554. Tel. +1-207 677 2494

Whaling Museum, 13 Broad Street, Nantucket, MA 0255. Tel. +1-508 228 1894

NETHERLANDS

Cultuur-historischmuseum 'Sorgdragen', Herenweg 1, 9161 AM Hollum-Ameland (Frise). Tel. + 31-(0)519 554477 **Museum 't Fiskershûske**, Fiskerspaed 4–8a, 9142 VN Moddergat (Frise). Tel. +31-(0)519 589454

The
HARBOUR
INN

RESTAURANT

PECHE
LA CODAILLE

THE
LOBSTER

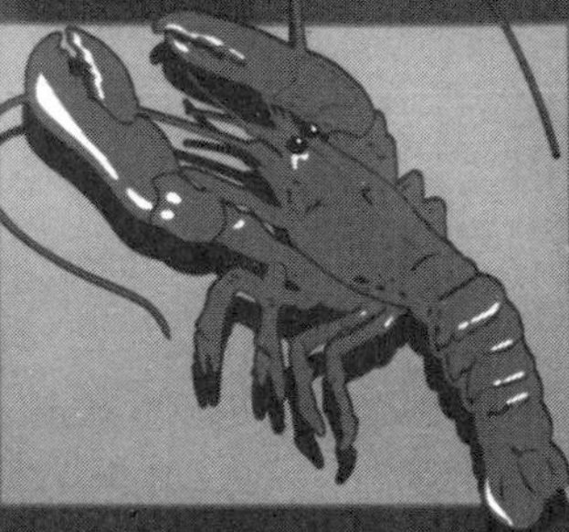

WET F
AVAILABLE F
PLEASE ASK FOR W
COD
HADDOCK
PLAICE
SKATE
DOVER SO
LEMON SOL
TURBOT
HALIBUT
MONKFISH
SALMON
SEA TROU
AINBOW
SHELLFISH
in shell and shelled
cockles/mussels/oysters
pink shrimps/brown shrimps
NORTH ATLANTIC PRAWNS
King Prawns (cooked)

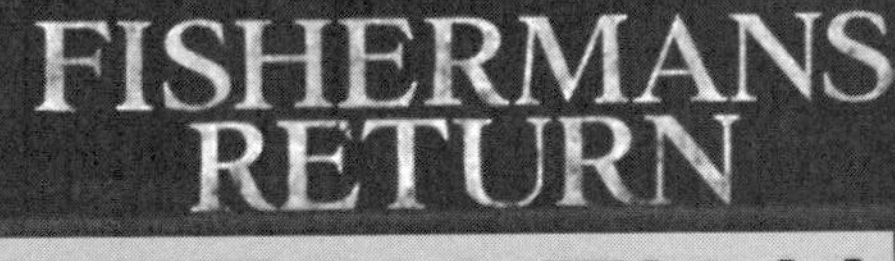
FISHERMANS
RETURN

ADNAMS
The
ANCHOR INN

DRIFTER

BISTRO
TEAROOMS
el. 01502 724806

FRESH FISH

La Moulerie